the new
Muffin
cook

Your Promise of Success

Welcome to the world of Confident Cooking, created for you in
our test kitchen, where recipes are double-tested by our team
of home economists to achieve a high standard of success.

Easy-bake muffins

Mmm... the aroma of freshly baked muffins is unbeatable. And all it takes is a few ingredients and some gentle mixing to create your own parcels of yumminess.

Plain muffins

2¹/2 cups (310 g) self-raising flour
³/4 cup (185 g) caster sugar
1¹/4 cups (315 ml) milk
2 eggs
1 teaspoon vanilla essence
100 g unsalted butter, melted and cooled

Low-fat muffins

2¹/2 cups (310 g) self-raising flour
¹/4 teaspoon bicarbonate of soda
³/4 cup (185 g) caster sugar
1 egg
¹/4 cup (60 ml) oil
1–2 teaspoons vanilla essence
1 cup (250 g) yoghurt

MIX AND MATCH YOUR TINS

The first (and easiest) step in making muffins is to choose your tins. In this book, we have used the 12 hole regular (100 ml) muffin tin, the 6 hole Texas (200 ml) muffin tin and the 12 hole mini (40 ml) muffin tin.

You can easily interchange muffin tins. For example, a recipe that makes 12 regular muffins can instead make 6 large (Texas) muffins or 48 mini muffins. Just remember to adjust the cooking time: add 5–10 minutes when cooking larger muffins and reduce it if making smaller muffins than the recipe specifies.

Although most tins are non-stick, lightly greasing them with melted butter or a mild-flavoured oil is a good idea for very sugary muffins because they are sticky. Alternatively, you can line the tins with muffin papers.

THE METHOD

The method is the same for all muffins, so once you have tried one, you can make hundreds of variations. To begin, preheat the oven to moderately hot 200°C (400°F/Gas 6), then lightly grease the muffin tin.

Sift the flour into a large bowl so that your muffins are light. Stir in any other dry

Choose your muffin tins from the range available, then lightly grease them.

Make a well in the centre of the dry ingredients and add the liquid.

ingredients, then make a well in the centre.

Place all the liquid ingredients in a jug, whisk together and pour into the well. Sometimes the butter will be added separately because it doesn't combine well with some ingredients. It helps if the butter is cooled slightly.

Fold the mixture gently with a metal spoon (a metal spoon cuts through the batter smoothly) until just combined. The mixture should be lumpy and coarse looking—don't keep stirring or the muffins will become tough and rubbery.

When the liquid is almost incorporated, gently fold in any other ingredients, such as fresh or dried fruit.

Next, divide the mixture evenly among the muffin holes and follow any topping and baking instructions.

COOKING POINTERS

When cooked, the muffins should have shrunk slightly away from the sides of the tin. The centre should be cooked. To test, insert a skewer in the centre of the muffins— if it comes out clean, they are ready.

Allow the muffins to cool for 5 minutes in the tins before loosening them with a flat-bladed knife and lifting them out onto a wire rack. The reason most muffins should be removed from the tin after a few minutes is that they will become soggy on the bottom. However, muffins with a soft filling benefit from a few extra minutes in the tin so that the filling can firm.

STORAGE AND FREEZING

In the unlikely event that you do have any muffins left over, store

them in an airtight container for up to 3 days. Alternatively, you can freeze muffins (without icing) for up to 3 months in sealed plastic bags or an airtight container; but it is hard to beat freshly baked muffins.

You can pop single frozen muffins in freezer bags and add them to lunch boxes— by the time they are ready to be eaten they will have thawed out.

AHEAD OF TIME

The plainer muffin mixtures, such as chocolate or blueberry or those without fillings, can be frozen uncooked in paper-lined muffin tins for up to 1 month, then removed from the freezer and baked in a preheated moderately hot (200°C/400°F/ Gas 6) oven for 25–30 minutes, or until golden and shrunk away from the sides.

Fold gently with a metal spoon until the mixture is just combined.

Bake until the muffins come away slightly from the side of the tin.

Muffins galore

Lunch-box stuffers, mid-morning snacks and delicious desserts—muffins are versatile enough to satisfy every craving.

Apple and berry crumble muffins

Preparation time:
  15 minutes
Total cooking time:
  25 minutes
Makes 12 regular muffins

1¹/4 cups (155 g) self-
  raising flour
1 cup (150 g) wholemeal
  self-raising flour
¹/4 teaspoon ground
  cinnamon
pinch ground cloves
¹/2 cup (115 g) firmly
  packed soft brown
  sugar
³/4 cup (185 ml) milk
2 eggs
125 g unsalted butter,
  melted and cooled
2 Granny Smith apples,
  peeled, cored, grated
1 cup (155 g) blueberries

Crumble
5 tablespoons plain
  flour
¹/4 cup (55 g) demerara
  sugar
¹/3 cup (35 g) rolled oats
40 g unsalted butter,
  chopped

1. Preheat the oven to moderately hot 190°C (375°F/Gas 5). Line 12 regular muffin holes with muffin papers. Sift the flours, cinnamon and cloves into a large bowl, add the husks and stir in the sugar. Make a well in the centre.
2. Put the milk, eggs and butter in a jug, whisk and pour into the well. Fold gently until just combined—the batter should be lumpy. Fold in the fruit. Divide among the muffin holes.
3. To make the crumble, put the flour, sugar and oats in a bowl. Rub the butter in with your fingertips until most of the lumps are gone. Sprinkle 2 teaspoons of the crumble over each muffin. Bake for 25 minutes, or until golden. Cool for 5 minutes, then transfer to a wire rack.

NUTRITION PER MUFFIN
Protein 4.5 g; Fat 13 g; Carbohydrate 40 g; Dietary Fibre 3 g; Cholesterol 37 mg; 1209 kJ (290 cal)

Apple and berry crumble muffins

Coffee nut muffins

Preparation time:
  20 minutes
Total cooking time:
  20 minutes
Makes 12 regular muffins

2 cups (250 g) self-
  raising flour
3/4 cup (140 g) soft
  brown sugar
1 1/4 cups (140 g)
  ground hazelnuts
1/4 cup (30 g) chopped
  roasted hazelnuts
1/4 cup (20 g) instant
  coffee
1 1/4 cups (315 ml)
  buttermilk
2 eggs
125 g unsalted butter,
  melted and cooled

1. Preheat the oven
to moderate 180°C
(350°F/ Gas 4). Line
12 regular muffin holes
with muffin papers. Sift
the flour into a large
bowl and add the sugar
and nuts. Make a well
in the centre.
2. Stir the coffee into
the buttermilk until
dissolved. Whisk in the
eggs and butter. Pour
into the well. Fold until
just combined—the
batter should be lumpy.
3. Divide among the
muffin holes. Bake for
20 minutes, or until a
skewer inserted in the
middle comes out clean.
Cool briefly, then
transfer to a wire rack
to cool completely.
Serve with Glossy
chocolate topping
(page 36).

NUTRITION PER MUFFIN
*Protein 5.5 g; Fat 18 g;
Carbohydrate 28 g; Dietary
Fibre 2.5 g; Cholesterol
30 mg; 1240 kJ (295 cal)*

Orange-frosted carrot muffins

Preparation time:
  20 minutes +
  30 minutes cooling
Total cooking time:
  40 minutes
Makes 12 Texas muffins

2 cups (250 g) self-
  raising flour
3/4 teaspoon mixed spice
1 teaspoon bicarbonate
  of soda
1 tablespoon ground
  almonds
3/4 cup (165 g)
  demerara sugar
1 tablespoon golden
  syrup
75 g unsalted butter
1/4 cup (60 ml) milk
3 eggs, lightly beaten
1 1/4 teaspoons vanilla
  essence
150 ml oil
2 2/3 cups (410 g) firmly
  packed grated carrot
2 cups (250 g) roughly
  chopped pecans

Frosting
180 g cream cheese
25 g unsalted butter,
  softened
3/4 teaspoon orange zest
1 1/2 tablespoons orange
  juice
1/2 cup (60 g) icing sugar

1. Preheat the oven
to moderate 180°C
(350°F/Gas 4). Grease
12 Texas muffin holes.
Sift the flour, spice and
bicarbonate of soda into
a large bowl and add
the almonds, sugar and
a pinch of salt. Make a
well in the centre.
2. Melt the golden
syrup and butter in a
small saucepan over
low heat. Remove from
the heat, cool, then stir
in the milk, egg, vanilla
and oil. Pour into the
well. Fold until just
combined—the batter
should be lumpy. Stir in
the carrot and pecans.
3. Divide among the
muffin holes. Bake for
30–35 minutes, or until
the muffins come away
from the side of the tin.
Cool for 5 minutes, then
transfer to a wire rack.
4. Put the cream cheese,
butter and zest in a
bowl and beat until
fluffy. Beat in the juice
and icing sugar. Chill
for 30 minutes, then
spread on the muffins.

NUTRITION PER MUFFIN
*Protein 7.5 g; Fat 42 g;
Carbohydrate 40 g; Dietary
Fibre 4 g; Cholesterol
80 mg; 2315 kJ (553 cal)*

---

*Coffee nut muffins (top) and
Orange-frosted carrot muffins*

Lemon and poppy seed muffins

Preparation time:
  15 minutes
Total cooking time:
  20 minutes
Makes 12 regular muffins

2¹/2 cups (310 g) self-
  raising flour
¹/4 cup (40 g) poppy
  seeds
1 cup (250 g) caster
  sugar
2 eggs
1 cup (250 g) sour cream
2 tablespoons finely
  grated lemon rind
¹/4 cup (60 ml) lemon
  juice
200 g cream cheese

1. Preheat the oven to moderate 180°C (350°F/Gas 4). Grease 12 regular muffin holes. Sift the flour into a bowl and add the seeds and ³/4 cup (185 g) of the caster sugar. Make a well in the centre.
2. Place the eggs, sour cream, lemon rind and 2 tablespoons of the juice in a jug, whisk together and pour into the well. Fold gently until combined—the batter should be lumpy.
3. Divide the mixture among the muffin holes. Bake for 20 minutes, or until the muffins come away from the side of the tin. Cool for 5 minutes, then transfer to a wire rack.
4. Put the cream cheese and remaining sugar and lemon juice in a bowl and beat well with electric beaters. Spread on the muffins.

NUTRITION PER MUFFIN
*Protein 5.5 g; Fat 15 g;
Carbohydrate 40 g; Dietary
Fibre 1 g; Cholesterol
73 mg; 1311 kJ (313 cal)*

Pear and muesli muffins

Preparation time:
  25 minutes +
  10 minutes standing
Total cooking time:
  35 minutes
Makes 12 regular muffins

1¹/2 cups (225 g)
  toasted muesli
1 tablespoon plain flour
¹/2 cup (125 g) caster
  sugar
90 g unsalted butter,
  melted
¹/2 cup (100 g) chopped
  dried pears
¹/2 cup (125 ml) orange
  juice
1 tablespoon finely
  grated orange rind
2 cups (250 g) self-
  raising flour
¹/2 teaspoon baking
  powder
1 cup (250 ml)
  buttermilk
¹/4 cup (60 ml) milk
¹/4 cup (90 g) honey

1. To make the topping, place ¹/2 cup (75 g) of the muesli, the plain flour and half the sugar in a small bowl and mix in 2 tablespoons of the butter until combined.
2. Preheat the oven to moderately hot 200°C (400°F/Gas 6). Grease 12 regular muffin holes. Put the pears in a large bowl and add the orange juice and rind. Leave for 10 minutes.
3. Sift the self-raising flour and baking powder into the bowl with the pears and add the remaining muesli and sugar. Make a well in the centre.
4. Whisk the buttermilk and milk together in a jug and pour into the well in the pear mixture. Combine the honey and remaining butter, then add to the well. Fold until combined—the batter should be lumpy.
5. Divide the batter among the muffin holes, then sprinkle on the topping. Bake for 30–35 minutes, or until the muffins come away from the side of the tin. Cool briefly, then transfer to a wire rack. Serve warm with butter.

NUTRITION PER MUFFIN
*Protein 5.5 g; Fat 10 g;
Carbohydrate 48 g; Dietary
Fibre 3 g; Cholesterol
22 mg; 1276 kJ (305 cal)*

*Lemon and poppy seed muffins (top) and
Pear and muesli muffins*

Apricot and pecan muffins

Preparation time:
15 minutes
Total cooking time:
35 minutes
Makes 6 Texas muffins

1 1/3 cups (245 g) dried
  apricots, roughly
  chopped
2 cups (250 g) self-
  raising flour
1/2 teaspoon
  bicarbonate of soda
60 g unsalted butter
1/3 cup (75 g) raw sugar
3/4 cup (90 g) coarsely
  chopped pecans
1/2 cup (125 ml) milk
1 egg
1/4 cup (60 ml) maple
  syrup
1/2 teaspoon vanilla
  essence

1. Preheat the oven to
moderate 180°C (350°F/
Gas 4). Grease 6 Texas
muffin holes. Place the
apricots and 1 cup
(250 ml) water in a
saucepan and bring to
the boil. Simmer for
10 minutes, or until
all the water has been
absorbed. Remove
from the heat.
2. Sift the flour and
bicarbonate of soda
into a large bowl. Rub
the butter in with your
fingertips until the
mixture resembles fine
breadcrumbs. Add the
sugar and pecans. Make
a well in the centre.
3. Place the milk, egg,
maple syrup and vanilla
in a jug, whisk together
and pour into the well.
Fold gently until just
combined—the batter
should be lumpy. Fold
in the apricots.
4. Divide the mixture
among the muffin
holes, then bake for
20–25 minutes, or until
the muffins come away
from the side of the
tin. Cool briefly, then
transfer to a wire rack.

NUTRITION PER MUFFIN
*Protein 8.5 g; Fat 20 g;
Carbohydrate 72 g; Dietary
Fibre 6.5 g; Cholesterol
55 mg; 2090 kJ (500 cal)*

Jam-filled muffins

Preparation time:
  20 minutes
Total cooking time:
  30 minutes
Makes 12 regular muffins

2 3/4 cups (340 g) self-
  raising flour
3/4 cup (185 g) caster
  sugar
1 cup (250 ml)
  buttermilk
1/4 cup (60 ml) milk
2 eggs
1 teaspoon vanilla
  essence
100 g unsalted butter,
  melted and cooled
200 g raspberries
1/3 cup (105 g)
  raspberry jam
100 g unsalted butter,
  melted, extra
1/2 cup (125 g) caster
  sugar, extra
1 teaspoon ground
  cinnamon

1. Preheat the oven to
moderately hot 200°C
(400°F/Gas 6). Grease
12 regular muffin holes.
Sift the flour into a bowl
and add the sugar. Make
a well in the centre.
2. Put the buttermilk,
milk, eggs, vanilla and
butter in a jug, whisk
together and pour into
the well. Fold until just
combined—the batter
should be lumpy. Fold
in the berries.
3. Divide the mixture
among the muffin holes.
Indent the centre of
each muffin and fill
with 1/2 teaspoon jam,
then cover with batter.
4. Bake the muffins for
25–30 minutes, or until
they come away from
the side of the tin. Cool
for 5 minutes, then
transfer to a wire rack.
5. Brush each muffin
all over with the extra
melted butter, then roll
in the combined extra
sugar and cinnamon.

NUTRITION PER MUFFIN
*Protein 6.5 g; Fat 17 g;
Carbohydrate 62 g; Dietary
Fibre 2 g; Cholesterol
80 mg; 1777 kJ (424 cal)*

*Apricot and pecan muffins (top) and
Jam-filled muffins*

Sticky date muffins

Preparation time:
  20 minutes +
  10 minutes standing
Total cooking time:
  30 minutes
Makes 12 regular muffins

1 cup (160 g) pitted
  dates, chopped
1 teaspoon bicarbonate
  of soda
90 g unsalted butter,
  softened
3/4 cup (165 g) firmly
  packed dark brown
  sugar
1 teaspoon vanilla
  essence
2 eggs
1¹/2 cups (185 g) self-
  raising flour
1/2 cup (60 g) plain flour
2/3 cup (170 ml) cream
2/3 cup (155 g) firmly
  packed dark brown
  sugar, extra
1/2 cup (60 g) chopped
  walnuts

1. Preheat the oven to
moderately hot 200°C
(400°F/Gas 6). Grease
12 regular muffin holes.
Put the dates and
1 cup (250 ml) water
in a bowl, then add the
bicarbonate of soda.
Leave for 10 minutes.
2. Put the butter, sugar
and vanilla in a bowl
and beat with electric
beaters. Add the eggs
one at a time, beating
well after each addition.
Stir in the date mixture,
then the sifted flours.
3. Divide the mixture
among the muffin holes.
Bake for 20–25 minutes,
or until the muffins
come away from the
side of the tin. Cool
slightly, then transfer
to a wire rack that is
sitting over a tray.
4. Meanwhile, put the
cream and extra sugar
in a small saucepan and
stir over low heat until
the sugar dissolves.
5. Brush the muffins
with sauce, sprinkle
with walnuts and serve.

NUTRITION PER MUFFIN
*Protein 4.5 g; Fat 17 g;
Carbohydrate 50 g; Dietary
Fibre 2.5 g; Cholesterol
68 mg; 1513 kJ (361 cal)*

Fig and oat bran muffins

Preparation time:
  15 minutes
Total cooking time:
  25 minutes
Makes 12 regular muffins

1 cup (125 g) self-
  raising flour
1/2 cup (75 g) wholemeal
  self-raising flour
1/2 teaspoon baking
  powder
1 cup (150 g) oat bran
1/4 cup (55 g) firmly
  packed soft brown
  sugar
1 cup (250 ml) milk
2 eggs
1/4 cup (90 g) golden
  syrup
60 g unsalted butter,
  melted and cooled
1 cup (185 g) soft dried
  figs, chopped
3 dried figs, cut into
  strips, extra

1. Preheat the oven to
moderately hot 200°C
(400°F/Gas 6). Grease
12 regular muffin
holes. Sift the flours
and baking powder
into a bowl, add the
husks, then the oat
bran and sugar. Make
a well in the centre.
2. Place the milk and
eggs in a jug, whisk
together and pour
into the well. Add the
combined golden syrup
and butter and fold
gently until just
combined—the batter
should be lumpy. Fold
in the chopped figs.
3. Divide the mixture
among the muffin holes
and top with the extra
strips of fig. Bake for
20–25 minutes, or until
the muffins come away
from the side of the
tin. Cool in the tin for
5 minutes, then transfer
to a wire rack.

NUTRITION PER MUFFIN
*Protein 6.5 g; Fat 7 g;
Carbohydrate 38 g; Dietary
Fibre 6 g; Cholesterol
45 mg; 956 kJ (228 cal)*

*Sticky date muffins (top) and
Fig and oat bran muffins*

Lime and coconut muffins

Preparation time:
25 minutes
Total cooking time:
25 minutes
Makes 12 regular muffins

2 cups (250 g) self-raising flour
1/2 cup (125 g) caster sugar
1 cup (90 g) desiccated coconut
2 teaspoons finely grated lime rind
1 cup (250 ml) milk
2 eggs
2 teaspoons vanilla essence
100 g unsalted butter, melted and cooled

1. Preheat the oven to moderately hot 200°C (400°F/Gas 6). Grease 12 regular muffin holes. Sift the flour into a bowl and add the sugar and coconut. Make a well in the centre.
2. Place the lime rind, milk, eggs, vanilla and butter in a jug, whisk and pour into the well. Fold gently until just combined—the batter should be lumpy.
3. Divide the mixture among the muffin holes. Bake for 20–25 minutes, or until the muffins come away from the

side of the tin.
4. Cool for 5 minutes, then transfer to a wire rack. Serve warm, drizzled with Lime syrup (page 37).

NUTRITION PER MUFFIN
Protein 4.5 g; Fat 14 g; Carbohydrate 27 g; Dietary Fibre 2 g; Cholesterol 55 mg; 1020 kJ (245 cal)

Hot cross muffins

Preparation time:
20 minutes
Total cooking time:
25 minutes
Makes 12 regular muffins

2 cups (250 g) self-raising flour
3 teaspoons ground cinnamon
125 g unsalted butter, chopped
1 cup (160 g) sultanas
1/4 cup (45 g) mixed peel
3/4 cup (185 g) caster sugar
3/4 cup (185 ml) milk
2 eggs, lightly beaten
2 teaspoons powdered gelatine
2 tablespoons caster sugar, extra
1/2 cup (60 g) icing sugar
2 teaspoons lemon juice

1. Preheat the oven to moderately hot 200°C (400°F/Gas 6). Grease 12 regular muffin holes. Sift the flour and

cinnamon into a large bowl, add the butter and rub it in with your fingertips until the mixture resembles fine breadcrumbs. Stir in the sultanas, peel and caster sugar. Make a well in the centre.
2. Place the milk and eggs in a jug, whisk and pour into the well. Fold gently until just combined—the batter should be lumpy.
3. Divide among the muffin holes. Bake for 20–25 minutes, or until the muffins come away from the side of the tin. Cool briefly, then transfer to a wire rack.
4. Meanwhile, to make the glaze, combine the gelatine, extra sugar and 2 tablespoons water in a small saucepan and stir over low heat for 1 minute, or until the sugar and gelatine are dissolved, then remove from the heat. Brush the warm muffins with the glaze a couple of times, then cool.
5. To make the icing, mix the icing sugar and lemon juice together until smooth. Spoon the icing into the corner of a small plastic bag, snip off the end and pipe a cross on each muffin and allow to set.

NUTRITION PER MUFFIN
Protein 4.5 g; Fat 10 g; Carbohydrate 32 g; Dietary Fibre 1.5 g; Cholesterol 58 mg; 998 kJ (238 cal)

Lime and coconut muffins (top) and Hot cross muffins

Almond, berry and yoghurt muffins

Preparation time:
  15 minutes
Total cooking time:
  20 minutes
Makes 12 regular muffins

1¹/2 cups (185 g) plain
  flour
3 teaspoons baking
  powder
1 cup (115 g) ground
  almonds
³/4 cup (185 g) caster
  sugar
2 eggs
125 g unsalted butter,
  melted and cooled
1 cup (250 g) Greek-
  style plain yoghurt
300 g blueberries
2 tablespoons flaked
  almonds

1. Preheat the oven
to moderate 180°C
(350°F/ Gas 4). Grease
12 regular muffin
holes. Sift the flour and
baking powder into a
large bowl and stir in
the ground almonds
and sugar. Make a
well in the centre.
2. Put the eggs, butter
and yoghurt in a jug,
whisk and pour into the
well. Fold gently until
combined—the batter
should be lumpy. Lightly
fold in the berries.
3. Divide the mixture
evenly among the
muffin holes. Top each
muffin with flaked
almonds. Bake for
20 minutes, or until the
muffins come away
from the side of the tin.
Cool for 5 minutes, then
transfer to a wire rack.

NUTRITION PER MUFFIN
*Protein 6 g; Fat 17 g;
Carbohydrate 30 g; Dietary
Fibre 2 g; Cholesterol
60 mg; 1252 kJ (299 cal)*

Chocolate muffins with a cream cheese centre

Preparation time:
  15 minutes
Total cooking time:
  20 minutes
Makes 12 regular muffins

Filling
100 g cream cheese,
  softened
2 tablespoons caster
  sugar
¹/2 teaspoon vanilla
  essence
90 g white chocolate
  melts, melted

2¹/4 cups (280 g) plain
  flour
¹/3 cup (40 g) cocoa
  powder
1 teaspoon bicarbonate
  of soda
²/3 cup (160 g) caster
  sugar
³/4 cup (185 ml) milk
1 teaspoon vanilla
  essence
³/4 cup (185 ml) oil
cocoa powder, to dust
icing sugar, to dust

1. Preheat the oven
to moderate 180°C
(350°F/Gas 4). Grease
12 regular muffin holes.
Blend the cream cheese,
sugar and vanilla in a
bowl with electric
beaters. Stir in the
melted chocolate.
2. Sift the flour, cocoa
and bicarbonate of
soda into a large bowl
and add the sugar. Make
a well in the centre.
3. Whisk the milk,
vanilla essence and oil
together in a jug and
pour into the well. Fold
gently until just
combined—the batter
should be lumpy.
4. Fill each muffin
hole one third full
with the batter. Place
a tablespoon of the
filling into each muffin
hole and top with the
remaining batter. Bake
for 20 minutes, or until
the muffins come away
from the side of the tin.
Cool briefly, then
transfer to a wire rack.
Dust with cocoa and
icing sugar. Serve warm.

NUTRITION PER MUFFIN
*Protein 5 g; Fat 20 g;
Carbohydrate 40 g; Dietary
Fibre 1 g; Cholesterol
12 mg; 1516 kJ (362 cal)*

*Almond, berry and yoghurt muffins (top) and
Chocolate muffins with a cream cheese centre*

Cappuccino ice cream muffins

Preparation time:
  30 minutes
Total cooking time:
  25 minutes
Makes 10 Texas muffins

185 g butter
1¹/3 cups (340 g) caster sugar
2¹/2 teaspoons vanilla essence
3 eggs
²/3 cup (85 g) self-raising flour
1³/4 cups (215 g) plain flour
1¹/2 teaspoons bicarbonate of soda
³/4 cup (90 g) cocoa powder
1 cup (250 ml) buttermilk
1 tablespoon instant coffee
1 litre vanilla ice cream
1 cup (250 ml) thick cream
1 tablespoon icing sugar
125 g dark chocolate melts, melted
cocoa powder, for dusting

1. Preheat the oven to moderate 180°C (350°F/Gas 4). Grease 10 Texas muffin holes. Beat the butter and sugar with electric beaters until light and creamy. Beat in the vanilla essence. Add the eggs, one at a time, beating well after each addition.
2. Sift the self-raising and plain flours, bicarbonate of soda and cocoa powder into a bowl. Fold into the butter and sugar mixture alternately with the buttermilk. Stir until just smooth.
3. Divide the mixture evenly among the muffin holes. Bake for about 25 minutes, or until a skewer comes out clean when inserted into the centre. Cool for 5 minutes, then transfer to a wire rack to cool completely.
4. Mix the coffee and 2 tablespoons boiling water in a small bowl or cup until dissolved, then cool. Roughly chop the ice cream in a large bowl and stir until thick and creamy. Add the coffee mixture and stir until just combined. Return to the freezer until required. Beat the cream and icing sugar with electric beaters until soft peaks form. Refrigerate until required.
5. Draw the outlines of 10 small spoons onto baking paper, then turn the paper over. Spoon the melted chocolate into a paper piping bag and pipe around the outlines of the spoons, then fill in the outlines. You will need to repeat this until you have piped 10 spoons. Allow the chocolate to set.
6. Cut a circle in the top of each muffin, leaving a 1 cm border around the edge. Using a spoon, scoop out the muffin from inside the circle, reserving the tops and leaving a 1 cm thick shell.
7. Stir the coffee ice cream with a spoon until it is softened, then scoop it into the muffins, so that it comes slightly above the top of each one. Replace the muffin tops, gently pressing them down onto the ice cream.
8. Spread the beaten cream roughly over the tops of the muffins to resemble the froth on the top of a cappuccino. Dust lightly with the cocoa and serve with a chocolate spoon.

NUTRITION PER MUFFIN
Protein 13 g; Fat 44 g; Carbohydrate 90 g; Dietary Fibre 2 g; Cholesterol 166 mg; 3333 kJ (796 cal)

Variation: For those people who can never get enough chocolate, use chocolate ice cream instead of vanilla to make a mochaccino ice cream muffin.

Cappuccino ice cream muffins

Hummingbird muffins

Preparation time:
  15 minutes + cooling
Total cooking time:
  30 minutes
Makes 12 regular muffins

1³/4 *cups (215 g) self-raising flour*
1¹/4 *cups (275 g) raw sugar*
2 *teaspoons ground cinnamon*
1 *cup (125 g) chopped pecans*
2 *eggs*
³/4 *cup (185 ml) oil*
2 *cups (480 g) mashed ripe banana*
¹/2 *cup (130 g) drained crushed pineapple*
6 *pecans, halved*

1. Preheat the oven to moderate 180°C (350°F/Gas 4). Line 12 regular muffin holes with muffin papers. Sift the flour into a bowl and stir in the sugar, cinnamon and pecans. Make a well in the centre.
2. Put the eggs and oil in a jug, whisk, then pour into the well. Add the banana and pineapple. Fold gently until just combined—the batter should be lumpy.
3. Divide among the muffin holes. Bake for 25–30 minutes, or until golden. Cool briefly, then transfer to a wire rack to cool completely.

4. Spread with Cream cheese icing (page 36). Top with pecan halves.

NUTRITION PER MUFFIN
Protein 4.5 g; Fat 24 g; Carbohydrate 46 g; Dietary Fibre 3 g; Cholesterol 30 mg; 1710 kJ (410 cal)

Rhubarb crumble muffins

Preparation time:
  15 minutes + cooling
Total cooking time:
  25 minutes
Makes 12 regular muffins

Crumble
40 *g unsalted butter, chopped*
¹/3 *cup (40 g) plain flour*
2 *tablespoons soft brown sugar*
2 *tablespoons flaked almonds*

250 *g rhubarb, cut into 1 cm pieces*
²/3 *cup (125 g) soft brown sugar*
1 *cup (125 g) plain flour*
¹/2 *cup (75 g) wholemeal plain flour*
2 *teaspoons baking powder*
¹/2 *cup (125 g) caster sugar*
¹/2 *cup (55 g) ground almonds*
¹/3 *cup (80 ml) milk*
1 *egg, lightly beaten*
75 *g unsalted butter, melted and cooled*

1. Preheat the oven to moderately hot 200°C (400°F/Gas 6). Grease 12 regular muffin holes. To make the crumble, put the butter and flour in a bowl and rub with your fingers until crumbly. Add the sugar and almonds.
2. Put the rhubarb, brown sugar and ¹/4 cup (60 ml) water in a small saucepan and cook over medium heat for 5 minutes, or until tender. Cool and drain.
3. Sift the flours and baking powder into a bowl and add the husks from the flour, the caster sugar and ground almonds. Stir, then make a well in the centre.
4. Put the milk, egg and butter in a jug, whisk together, then pour into the well. Fold gently until just combined—the batter should be lumpy. Fold in the rhubarb.
5. Divide the mixture among the muffin holes and sprinkle with the crumble. Bake for 20 minutes, or until the muffins come away from the side of the tin. Cool for 5 minutes, then transfer to a wire rack.

NUTRITION PER MUFFIN
Protein 3.5 g; Fat 13 g; Carbohydrate 31 g; Dietary Fibre 2 g; Cholesterol 40 mg; 1030 kJ (245 cal)

Hummingbird muffins (top) and Rhubarb crumble muffins

Pear and hazelnut bran muffins

Preparation time:
  10 minutes +
  overnight refrigeration
Total cooking time:
  30 minutes
Makes 6 Texas muffins

250 g dried pears,
  chopped
2 cups (140 g)
  processed bran cereal
2 cups (500 ml) milk
1^1/$_3$ cups (310 g) firmly
  packed soft brown
  sugar
2 tablespoons maple
  syrup
2 cups (250 g) self-
  raising flour
180 g roasted
  hazelnuts, chopped
1 teaspoon ground
  cinnamon
1 teaspoon caster sugar

1. Mix the pears,
cereal, milk, brown
sugar and maple syrup
together in a large
bowl, then cover and
refrigerate overnight.
2. Preheat the oven
to moderate 180°C
(350°F/Gas 4). Grease
6 Texas muffin holes.
Sift the flour into the
cereal mixture and add
the nuts. Fold gently
until combined—the
batter should be lumpy.
3. Divide the mixture
among the muffin holes.
Bake for 30 minutes, or
until the muffins come
away from the side
of the tin. Cool for
5 minutes, then transfer
to a wire rack. Sprinkle
with the combined
cinnamon and sugar.
Serve buttered.

NUTRITION PER MUFFIN
*Protein 17 g; Fat 23 g;
Carbohydrate 114 g; Dietary
Fibre 20 g; Cholesterol
11 mg; 3025 kJ (723 cal)*

Oat and golden syrup muffins

Preparation time:
  10 minutes
Total cooking time:
  25 minutes
Makes 12 regular muffins

Topping
^{1}/$_2$ cup (50 g) oats
^{1}/$_3$ cup (80 g) firmly
  packed soft brown
  sugar
^{1}/$_3$ cup (30 g)
  desiccated coconut
40 g unsalted butter,
  chopped

2^1/$_2$ cups (310 g) self-
  raising flour
2 teaspoons baking
  powder
^{1}/$_2$ cup (115 g) firmly
  packed soft brown
  sugar
1 cup (250 ml)
  buttermilk
2 eggs, lightly beaten
2 teaspoons vanilla
  essence
100 g unsalted butter,
  chopped
^{1}/$_3$ cup (115 g) golden
  syrup

1. Preheat the oven to
moderately hot 200°C
(400°F/Gas 6). Grease
12 regular muffin
holes. To make the
topping, place the oats,
sugar and coconut in a
bowl and mix together.
Add the butter and rub
it in with your fingertips
until crumbly.
2. Sift the flour and
baking powder into a
bowl and stir in the
sugar. Make a well
in the centre.
3. Whisk the buttermilk,
eggs and vanilla
together in a jug and
pour into the well.
4. Melt the butter and
golden syrup in a small
saucepan over low
heat. Pour into the
well. Fold gently until
just combined—the
batter should be lumpy.
5. Divide the mixture
among the muffin
holes, then sprinkle on
the topping. Bake for
20–25 minutes, or until
the muffins come away
from the side of the tin.
Cool briefly, then
transfer to a wire rack.

NUTRITION PER MUFFIN
*Protein 5 g; Fat 13 g;
Carbohydrate 45 g; Dietary
Fibre 1.5 g; Cholesterol
60 mg; 1316 kJ (314 cal)*

*Pear and hazelnut bran muffins (top) and
Oat and golden syrup muffins*

All the old favourites

For the following classic muffins, preheat the oven to moderately hot 200°C (400°F/Gas 6) and lightly grease 48 mini muffin holes. The mixture can make 12 regular or 6 Texas muffins instead.

Blueberry muffins

Sift 2^1/2 cups (310 g) self-raising flour and ^{1}/4 teaspoon ground cinnamon into a large bowl and stir in ^{3}/4 cup (185 g) caster sugar. Make a well in the centre.

Put 1^1/2 cups (375 ml) milk, 2 eggs, 1 teaspoon vanilla essence and 150 g melted and cooled unsalted butter in a jug and whisk. Pour into the well. Fold gently until just combined—the batter should be lumpy. Gently fold in 200 g blueberries.

Divide the mixture evenly among the muffin holes. Bake for 20–25 minutes, or until the muffins come away slightly from the side of the tin. Cool, then transfer to a wire rack.

Bran muffins

Sift 1^2/3 cups (210 g) self-raising flour into a large bowl and stir in 1 cup (75 g) unprocessed bran, 1^1/2 cups (240 g) sultanas and ^{1}/3 cup (90 g) caster sugar. Make a well in the centre.

Pour 1^1/2 cups (375 ml) milk, 2 eggs and 100 g melted and cooled unsalted butter into a large jug, whisk and pour into the well. Fold gently until just combined—the batter should be lumpy.

Divide the mixture among the muffin holes. Bake for 20–25 minutes, or until the muffins come away from the side of the tin. Cool for 5 minutes, then transfer to a wire rack.

Chocolate muffins

Sift 2¹/2 cups (310 g) self-raising flour, ¹/3 cup (40 g) cocoa powder and ¹/2 teaspoon bicarbonate of soda into a large bowl, then stir in ²/3 cup (160 g) caster sugar and 1 cup (175 g) choc bits. Make a well in the centre.

Place 1 cup (250 ml) buttermilk, 2 eggs and 150 g melted and cooled unsalted butter in a large jug, mix and pour into the well. Fold gently until just combined—the batter should be lumpy.

Divide the mixture among the muffin holes. Bake for 20–25 minutes, or until the muffins come away from the side of the tin. Cool for 5 minutes, then lift out onto a wire rack.

Apple and cinnamon muffins

Place a 400 g can of pie apple in a bowl and break up with a knife.

Sift 2¹/2 cups (310 g) self-raising flour and 2 teaspoons ground cinnamon into a large bowl. Add ²/3 cup (125 g) soft brown sugar and ¹/2 cup (60 g) finely chopped walnuts, stir together and make a well in the centre.

Place 1¹/3 cups (330 ml) milk, 2 eggs, 1 teaspoon vanilla essence and 150 g melted and cooled unsalted butter in a jug, whisk together and pour into the well. Add the apples, then fold gently until just combined—the batter should be lumpy.

Divide the mixture evenly among the muffin holes. Bake for 20–25 minutes, or until the muffins come away slightly from the side of the tin. Cool for 5 minutes, then transfer to a wire rack.

Note: Dress up these muffins by adding a topping. Try Blueberry muffins with Lemon glaze, Bran muffins with Cream cheese icing, Chocolate muffins with Cappuccino swirl icing or Apple and cinnamon muffins with Apricot glaze (pages 36–37).

From left: Blueberry; Bran; Chocolate; Apple and cinnamon.

Macadamia and mango muffins

Preparation time:
  15 minutes
Total cooking time:
  30 minutes
Makes 6 Texas muffins

2¹/4 cups (280 g) self-
  raising flour
¹/2 cup (110 g) raw
  sugar
¹/2 cup (80 g)
  macadamia nuts,
  toasted and roughly
  chopped
125 g unsalted butter,
  chopped
2 tablespoons honey
425 g can mango slices
  in syrup, drained
²/3 cup (170 ml) milk
1 egg, lightly beaten

1. Preheat the oven to moderately hot 190°C (375°F/Gas 5). Line 6 Texas muffin holes with muffin papers. Sift the flour into a large bowl, then add the sugar and macadamias. Make a well in the centre.
2. Melt the butter and honey in a small saucepan over low heat until the butter has dissolved, then pour into a jug. Purée the mango slices in a food processor or blender until smooth and add to the jug. Add the milk and egg, mix together and pour into the well in the dry ingredients.

Fold gently until just combined—the batter should be lumpy.
3. Divide the muffin mixture evenly among the muffin holes. Bake for 20–25 minutes, or until golden brown. Cool for 5 minutes, then transfer to a wire rack. Serve slightly warm with butter and honey or apricot jam.

NUTRITION PER MUFFIN
Protein 8 g; Fat 28 g; Carbohydrate 75 g; Dietary Fibre 3 g; Cholesterol 80 mg; 2421 kJ (580 cal)

Lemon syrup muffins

Preparation time:
  20 minutes
Total cooking time:
  20 minutes
Makes 12 regular muffins

2¹/2 cups (310 g) self-
  raising flour
1¹/4 cups (310 g) caster
  sugar
¹/2 cup (125 g) plain
  yoghurt
¹/3 cup (80 ml) milk
1 egg
1 cup (250 ml) lemon
  juice
2¹/4 tablespoons finely
  grated lemon rind
110 g unsalted butter,
  melted and cooled
¹/4 cup (60 g) ready-
  made lemon butter

1. Preheat the oven to moderately hot 200°C (400°F/Gas 6). Grease 12 regular muffin holes. Sift the flour into a large bowl and add ³/4 cup (185 g) sugar and mix together. Make a well in the centre.
2. Put the yoghurt, milk, egg, half the lemon juice and 1¹/4 tablespoons of the lemon rind in a jug, whisk together and pour into the well. Add the butter. Fold gently until combined—the batter should be lumpy.
3. Divide half the batter among the muffin holes. Put 1 teaspoon of lemon butter in the centre of each, then cover with the remaining batter. Bake for 20 minutes, or until they come away from the side of the tin. Cool for 5 minutes.
4. Meanwhile, to make the syrup, place the remaining sugar, juice and rind in a small saucepan. Stir over medium heat until the sugar dissolves, then simmer for 5 minutes. Keep hot.
5. Place the muffins on a wire rack with a tray underneath and drizzle with syrup. Serve warm.

NUTRITION PER MUFFIN
Protein 4 g; Fat 10 g; Carbohydrate 50 g; Dietary Fibre 1 g; Cholesterol 45 mg; 1243 kJ (297 cal)

Macadamia and mango muffins (top) and Lemon syrup muffins

Marsala date muffins

Preparation time:
  20 minutes +
  10 minutes soaking
Total cooking time:
  20 minutes
Makes 12 regular muffins

1 egg
1/3 cup (80 ml) Marsala
1/4 cup (60 ml) oil
1 cup (160 g) chopped
  dates
2 cups (250 g) self-
  raising flour
1/4 teaspoon baking
  powder
195 g raw sugar
1 cup (125 g) chopped
  walnuts

1. Combine the egg, Marsala and oil in a bowl and add the dates. Leave, covered, for 10 minutes.
2. Preheat the oven to moderate 180°C (350°F/Gas 4). Line 12 regular muffin holes with muffin papers. Sift the flour and baking powder into a bowl and stir in the sugar, nuts and 1/4 teaspoon salt. Make a well in the centre.
3. Add the date mixture to the well. Fold until just combined—the batter should be lumpy.
4. Divide the mixture evenly among the muffin holes. Bake for 20 minutes, or until lightly browned. Cool for 5 minutes, then transfer to a wire rack.
5. Brush the warm muffins with Coffee glaze (page 37).

NUTRITION PER MUFFIN
Protein 4.5 g; Fat 13 g; Carbohydrate 40 g; Dietary Fibre 3 g; Cholesterol 15 mg; 1200 kJ (285 cal)

Pumpkin and walnut muffins

Preparation time:
  30 minutes
Total cooking time:
  30 minutes
Makes 12 regular muffins

375 g pumpkin, peeled
  and roughly chopped
2 1/2 cups (310 g) self-
  raising flour
2 teaspoons mixed spice
1/2 cup (60 g) chopped
  walnuts
3/4 cup (165 g) firmly
  packed soft brown
  sugar
1 cup (250 ml)
  buttermilk
2 eggs
90 g unsalted butter,
  melted and cooled
3/4 cup (90 g) icing sugar
1/3 cup (80 ml) maple
  syrup
1 tablespoon chopped
  walnuts, extra

1. Preheat the oven to moderately hot 200°C (400°F/Gas 6). Line 12 regular muffin holes with muffin papers. Steam the chopped pumpkin for 10 minutes, or until tender. Mash well and set aside until it has cooled.
2. Sift the flour and mixed spice into a large bowl and stir in the walnuts and brown sugar. Make a well in the centre.
3. Place the buttermilk, eggs and butter in a jug, whisk together and pour into the well. Fold gently until just combined—the batter should be lumpy. Fold in the pumpkin.
4. Divide the mixture evenly among the muffin holes. Bake for 20 minutes, or until golden. Cool for 5 minutes, then transfer to a wire rack to cool a little.
5. Meanwhile, to make the icing, put the icing sugar and maple syrup in a small bowl and stir until a brushable paste forms. Brush the icing all over the warm muffins, sprinkle with the extra walnuts, then cool. The icing will set as the muffins cool.

NUTRITION PER MUFFIN
Protein 6 g; Fat 12 g; Carbohydrate 50 g; Dietary Fibre 1.5 g; Cholesterol 50 mg; 1368 kJ (327 cal)

Pumpkin and walnut muffins (top) and Marsala date muffins

Ebony and ivory muffins

Preparation time:
20 minutes
Total cooking time:
20 minutes
Makes 12 regular muffins

2 cups (250 g) plain flour
1 tablespoon baking powder
1/3 cup (90 g) caster sugar
1 cup (250 g) vanilla yoghurt
2 eggs
125 g unsalted butter, melted and cooled
180 g dark cooking chocolate, melted
1/2 cup (60 g) chopped walnuts
1/2 cup (80 g) chopped blanched almonds
2 teaspoons finely grated orange rind

1. Preheat the oven to moderately hot 200°C (400°F/Gas 6). Grease 12 regular muffin holes. Sift the flour and baking powder into a large bowl and add the sugar and a pinch of salt. Stir, then make a well in the centre. Combine the yoghurt, eggs and butter, then pour into the well.
2. Fold gently until just combined—the batter should be lumpy. Transfer half the batter to another bowl.
3. Fold the chocolate and walnuts into one bowl of batter and the almonds and orange rind into the other.
4. Spoon chocolate batter into one side of each muffin hole and almond batter into the other side. Bake for 20 minutes, or until the muffins come away from the side of the tin. Cool for 5 minutes, then transfer to a wire rack.

NUTRITION PER MUFFIN
Protein 7 g; Fat 22 g; Carbohydrate 34 g; Dietary Fibre 2 g; Cholesterol 59.5 mg; 1496 kJ (357 cal)

Strawberry and ice cream muffins

Preparation time:
25 minutes + cooling
Total cooking time:
35 minutes
Makes 6 Texas muffins

1 1/2 cups (185 g) self-raising flour
1/2 cup (55 g) ground almonds
1/2 cup (125 g) caster sugar
1 cup (250 ml) milk
2 eggs
3 teaspoons vanilla essence
100 g unsalted butter, melted and cooled
200 g strawberries, sliced lengthways
1 tablespoon sugar
1 tablespoon Cointreau
3 vanilla ice cream slices, halved

1. Preheat the oven to moderately hot 200°C (400°F/Gas 6). Grease 6 Texas muffin holes. Sift the flour into a bowl and stir in the almonds and sugar. Make a well in the centre.
2. Place the milk, eggs and vanilla in a jug, whisk together and pour into the well. Add the melted butter. Fold gently until just combined—the batter should be lumpy.
3. Divide evenly among the muffin holes. Bake for 30–35 minutes, or until the muffins come away slightly from the side of the tin. Cool for 5 minutes, then transfer to a wire rack. Cool.
4. Meanwhile, put the strawberries in a bowl and sprinkle with the sugar and Cointreau. When the muffins are completely cool, split in half horizontally and place half a slice of ice cream on the muffin base, top with some berries and angle the muffin lid on top.

NUTRITION PER MUFFIN
Protein 9.5 g; Fat 24 g; Carbohydrate 52 g; Dietary Fibre 2.5 g; Cholesterol 112 mg; 1887 kJ (450 cal)

Ebony and ivory muffins (top) and Strawberry and ice cream muffins

Lemon meringue muffins

Preparation time:
  30 minutes +
  20 minutes cooling
Total cooking time:
  20 minutes
Makes 12 regular muffins

1³/4 cups (215 g) self-
  raising flour
³/4 cup (185 g) caster
  sugar
1 egg
1 egg yolk
²/3 cup (170 ml) milk
¹/2 teaspoon vanilla
  essence
90 g unsalted butter,
  melted and cooled
²/3 cup (200 g) ready-
  made lemon curd
2 egg whites
1 teaspoon caster sugar,
  extra

1. Preheat the oven to moderately hot 200°C (400°F/Gas 6). Lightly grease 12 regular muffin holes. Sift the flour into a large bowl and stir in ¹/4 cup (60 g) of the caster sugar. Make a well in the centre.
2. Place the egg and egg yolk in a bowl and add a pinch of salt. Beat the egg mixture together, then stir in the milk, vanilla essence and butter. Pour the egg mixture into the well in the dry ingredients. Fold gently until just combined—the batter should be lumpy.
3. Divide the muffin mixture evenly among the muffin holes. Bake for 15 minutes—the muffins will only rise a little way up the muffin holes. (Leave the oven on at the same temperature.)
4. Cool the muffins in the tin for 10 minutes, then loosen with a knife but leave in the tin. Hollow out the centre of each muffin with a melon baller, being careful not to pierce through the base of the muffins.
5. Stir the lemon curd well, then spoon the curd into a piping bag fitted with a 1.25 cm plain nozzle. Carefully pipe the curd into the hollowed-out centre of each muffin.
6. Whisk the egg whites in a clean dry bowl until stiff peaks form. Add a quarter of the remaining sugar at a time, beating well after each addition until stiff and glossy peaks form.
7. Place a heaped tablespoon of the meringue mixture on top of each muffin and form peaks with the back of a spoon.

Sprinkle a little of the extra caster sugar over the meringue on top of each muffin.
8. Return the muffins to the oven for 5 minutes, or until the meringue is lightly golden and crisp and the muffins come away slightly from the side of the tin. Cool in the tin for 10 minutes, then carefully transfer to a wire rack. Serve warm or at room temperature. These muffins are best eaten on the same day that they are made so that the meringue stays crispy.

NUTRITION PER MUFFIN
Protein 4.5 g; Fat 11 g; Carbohydrate 38 g; Dietary Fibre 0.5 g; Cholesterol 67 mg; 1105 kJ (265 cal)

Notes: Buy good-quality lemon curd or make your own. Ready-made lemon curd is available from supermarkets, delicatessens and gourmet food stores.

The meringue topping might come off the muffins when they first come out of the oven, but it will adhere as they cool—so handle the muffins carefully until completely cool.
Variation: You can also use other flavours of citrus curds, such as lime or orange to fill the muffins.

Lemon meringue muffins

Berry bran muffins with honey butter

Preparation time:
  25 minutes
Total cooking time:
  25 minutes
Makes 12 regular muffins

125 g unsalted butter,
  softened
1 tablespoon honey
1 cup (70 g) processed
  bran cereal
1¹/2 cups (375 ml) milk
2¹/4 cups (280 g) self-
  raising flour
¹/4 cup (60 g) caster
  sugar
1 egg, lightly beaten
¹/4 cup (90 g) honey
60 g unsalted butter,
  melted and cooled,
  extra
100 g strawberries,
  chopped
125 g raspberries

1. Beat the butter and honey together until fluffy. Chill until needed.
2. Preheat the oven to moderately hot 200°C (400°F/Gas 6). Grease 12 regular muffin holes. Put the cereal and milk in a large bowl and soak for 5 minutes.
3. Sift the flour into the bowl and stir in the sugar. Make a well in the centre. Mix the egg, honey and extra butter in a jug, then pour into the well. Fold gently until combined—the batter should be lumpy. Fold in the berries.
4. Divide the mixture among the muffin holes. Bake for 20–25 minutes, or until the muffins come away from the side of the tin. Cool for 5 minutes, then transfer to a wire rack. Serve with honey butter.

NUTRITION PER MUFFIN
Protein 15 g; Fat 23 g; Carbohydrate 35 g; Dietary Fibre 2.5 g; Cholesterol 340 mg; 1655 kJ (395 cal)

Apple muffins with a walnut streusel topping

Preparation time:
  20 minutes
Total cooking time:
  20 minutes
Makes 12 regular muffins

¹/3 cup (40 g) chopped
  walnuts
¹/4 cup (45 g) soft
  brown sugar
40 g unsalted butter,
  softened
2 cups (250 g) plain
  flour
3 teaspoons baking
  powder
1¹/2 teaspoons ground
  cinnamon
¹/2 teaspoon mixed spice
¹/2 cup (125 g) caster
  sugar
2/3 cup (170 ml) milk
2 eggs
1 teaspoon vanilla
  essence
125 g unsalted butter,
  melted and cooled,
  extra
2 Granny Smith apples,
  peeled, cored, diced

1. Preheat the oven to moderate 180°C (350°F/Gas 4). Grease 12 regular muffin holes. To make the topping, mix the walnuts, brown sugar and butter together in a bowl until a paste forms. Set aside.
2. Sift the flour, baking powder, cinnamon and mixed spice into a large bowl. Stir in the sugar. Make a well in the centre. Place the milk, eggs, vanilla and melted butter in a jug, whisk together and pour into the well. Fold gently until just combined— the batter should be lumpy. Fold in the apple.
3. Divide the mixture among the muffin holes. Gently press the topping into the batter. Bake for 20 minutes, or until the muffins come away from the side of the tin. Cool slightly, then transfer to a wire rack.

NUTRITION PER MUFFIN
Protein 4.5 g; Fat 15.5 g; Carbohydrate 34 g; Dietary Fibre 1.5 g; Cholesterol 66.5 mg; 1191 kJ (285 cal)

Berry bran muffins with honey butter (top) and Apple muffins with a walnut streusel topping

Icings and other toppings

There are no rules about which toppings go with which muffins—have fun experimenting and see what you come up with. All the toppings make enough for 12 regular, 48 mini or 6 Texas muffins.

Cream cheese icing

Combine 75 g spreadable cream cheese, 45 g butter and 1^1/2 teaspoons vanilla essence in a bowl and beat together until light and fluffy. Gradually beat in 1^1/2 cups (185 g) icing sugar and continue beating until the mixture is smooth. Spread the icing over cooled muffins.

Glossy chocolate topping

Chop 200 g dark chocolate into even-sized pieces and put in a heatproof bowl. Bring a saucepan of water to the boil, then remove the pan from the heat. Sit the bowl over the pan, making sure the base of the bowl does not sit in the water. Stir occasionally until the chocolate melts, then

remove from the heat. Quickly stir in ^{1}/2 cup (125 g) sour cream. If the chocolate starts to set, sit the bowl over the saucepan, stirring until dissolved. Add ^{1}/2 cup (60 g) icing sugar, stirring well. Swirl over cooled muffins and decorate with chocolate curls.

Cappuccino swirl

Dissolve 3 teaspoons instant espresso coffee powder in 1 teaspoon boiling water and allow

From left: Cream cheese icing; Glossy chocolate topping; Cappuccino swirl; Lime syrup; Apricot glaze.

to cool. Beat 90 g soft unsalted butter, 2 cups (250 g) icing sugar and 1 tablespoon milk with electric beaters until fluffy. Remove one third of the mixture and stir the dissolved coffee into the remaining mixture. Spread the coffee icing over cooled muffins, top with a swirl of white icing and dust with sifted cocoa.

Lime syrup

Put $^1/_2$ cup (125 g) sugar and 1 cup (250 ml) water in a small saucepan and stir over medium heat until dissolved. Add 1 stem thinly sliced lemon grass (white part only) and 4 kaffir lime leaves and bring to the boil.

Reduce the heat and simmer for 10 minutes, then remove from the heat. Add 2 tablespoons lime juice, then cool. Strain. Brush over warm muffins and garnish with lime zest.

Glazes

For a basic glaze, sift 1 cup (125 g) icing sugar into a bowl, then gradually add $1^1/_2$ tablespoons water and $^1/_2$ teaspoon vanilla essence and beat until the icing sugar dissolves and the mixture is smooth.

To make variations, use 1 cup (125 g) sifted icing sugar, add the flavouring and beat until smooth. Brush the glaze evenly over the muffins.

Variations
Coffee glaze: Dissolve 3 teaspoons instant coffee in 2 tablespoons water. Add 1 tablespoon cream and stir smooth. Stir into the icing sugar.
Apricot glaze: Combine 2 tablespoons apricot jam, 1 tablespoon lemon juice and $2^1/_2$ tablespoons water in a saucepan and warm gently. Sieve into the icing sugar and stir.
Lemon glaze: Combine the icing sugar, 1 teaspoon butter, ½ teaspoon lemon rind, 1 tablespoon lemon juice and 2 teaspoons water in a bowl. Bring a saucepan of water to the boil, remove from the heat and place the bowl over the pan and stir until spreadable.

Double chocolate chip muffins

Preparation time:
  15 minutes
Total cooking time:
  25 minutes
Makes 12 regular muffins

2¹/2 cups (310 g) self-
  raising flour
¹/2 cup (60 g) cocoa
  powder
¹/2 teaspoon
  bicarbonate of soda
³/4 cup (165 g) firmly
  packed soft brown
  sugar
1 cup (175 g) milk choc
  bits
1 cup (175 g) white
  choc bits or chopped
  white choc melts
1¹/4 cups (315 ml) milk
2 eggs
100 g unsalted butter,
  melted and cooled

1. Preheat the oven to
moderately hot 200°C
(400°F/Gas 6). Grease
12 regular muffin holes.
Sift the flour, cocoa and
bicarbonate of soda
into a large bowl and
stir in the sugar and
³/4 cup (130 g) each
of the choc bits. Make
a well in the centre.
2. Whisk together the
milk, eggs and butter in
a jug and pour into the
well. Fold gently—the
batter should be lumpy.

3. Divide the batter
among the muffin holes.
Sprinkle with the
remaining choc bits and
bake for 20–25 minutes,
or until the muffins
come away from the side
of the tin. Cool, then
transfer to a wire rack.

NUTRITION PER MUFFIN
*Protein 9 g; Fat 22 g;
Carbohydrate 60 g; Dietary
Fibre 1.5 g; Cholesterol
62 mg; 1960 kJ (470 cal)*

Orange and almond muffins with citrus syrup

Preparation time:
  20 minutes
Total cooking time:
  30 minutes
Makes 6 Texas muffins

³/4 cup (90 g) self-
  raising flour
³/4 cup (185 g) caster
  sugar
2¹/4 cups (255 g)
  ground almonds
¹/2 cup (125 ml) milk
2 eggs, separated
2 teaspoons finely
  grated orange rind
125 g unsalted butter,
  melted and cooled
2 tablespoons caster
  sugar, extra
³/4 cup (185 ml) orange
  juice
2 x 5 cm strips orange
  rind, extra

¹/2 cup (125 g) caster
  sugar, extra

1. Preheat the oven to
moderately hot 200°C
(400°F/Gas 6). Grease
6 Texas muffin holes.
Sift the flour into a bowl
and stir in the sugar
and almonds. Make
a well in the centre.
2. Combine the milk,
egg yolks, rind and
butter in a jug and pour
into the well. Fold until
just combined—the
batter should be lumpy.
3. Whisk the egg whites
in a clean dry bowl
until soft peaks form.
Gradually add the extra
sugar, beating well after
each addition until the
sugar dissolves. Gently
fold the egg white into
the batter in 2 batches.
4. Divide among the
muffin holes. Bake for
25–30 minutes, or until
the muffins come away
from the side of the tin.
Cool briefly, then
transfer to a baking tray.
5. Meanwhile, to make
the syrup, put the
orange juice, extra rind
and sugar in a small
saucepan and stir over
low heat until the sugar
dissolves, then simmer
for 2 minutes. Remove
the rind. Pour syrup
over the warm muffins
so they soak it up.

NUTRITION PER MUFFIN
*Protein 13 g; Fat 43 g;
Carbohydrate 74 g; Dietary
Fibre 4.5 g; Cholesterol
115 mg; 3045 kJ (727 cal)*

*Orange and almond muffins with citrus syrup
(top) and Double chocolate chip muffins*

Sticky gingerbread muffins

Preparation time:
20 minutes
Total cooking time:
30 minutes
Makes 12 regular muffins

2 cups (250 g) self-
raising flour
3/4 cup (90 g) plain
flour
1/2 teaspoon
bicarbonate of soda
3 teaspoons ground
ginger
1 teaspoon ground
cinnamon
1 teaspoon mixed spice
1 cup (230 g) firmly
packed soft brown
sugar
1/4 cup (55 g) chopped
glacé ginger
2/3 cup (235 g) golden
syrup
100 g unsalted butter,
chopped
1 cup (250 ml)
buttermilk
1 egg, lightly beaten

Ginger frosting
60 g unsalted butter,
softened
1 1/2 tablespoons golden
syrup
1 cup (125 g) icing
sugar
1/2 teaspoon ground
ginger
50 g dark chocolate,
chopped into even-
sized pieces

1. Preheat the oven to moderately hot 200°C (400°F/Gas 6). Grease 12 regular muffin holes. Sift the self-raising and plain flours, bicarbonate of soda, ground ginger, ground cinnamon and mixed spice into a large bowl and stir in the brown sugar and glacé ginger. Make a well in the centre.
2. Place the golden syrup and butter in a small saucepan and stir over medium heat until melted and well mixed. Remove from the heat and cool.
3. Combine the golden syrup mixture, buttermilk and egg in a large jug, mix together and pour into the well in the dry ingredients. Fold gently until just combined—the batter should be lumpy.
4. Divide the mixture evenly among the muffin holes. Bake for 20–25 minutes, or until the muffins come away from the side of the tin. Cool for 5 minutes in the tin, then transfer to a wire rack to cool completely.
5. To make the ginger frosting, beat the butter, golden syrup, icing sugar and ground ginger together with electric beaters in a bowl until light and fluffy. Spread evenly over the top of the cooled muffins.
6. Place the chocolate pieces in a heatproof bowl. Bring a saucepan of water to the boil, then remove from the heat. Sit the bowl over the saucepan, making sure the base of the bowl does not sit in the water. Stir occasionally until the chocolate has melted. Cool for 5 minutes.
7. Spoon the melted chocolate into the corner of a plastic sandwich bag. Snip off just the tip of the filled corner to create a nozzle. Pipe the chocolate over the icing in thin criss-crossing lines. Apply even pressure and move at a steady speed to prevent the chocolate from clumping. Allow the chocolate to set before serving the muffins.

NUTRITION PER MUFFIN
Protein 4.5 g; Fat 13 g; Carbohydrate 70 g; Dietary Fibre 1 g; Cholesterol 50 mg; 1730 kJ (413 cal)

Variations: If you prefer a milder flavoured frosting, you could use milk chocolate instead of the dark chocolate.
   Another delicious topping idea is the Apricot or Lemon glaze (page 37).

Sticky gingerbread muffins

Banana, oat and raisin muffins

Preparation time:
  25 minutes +
  15 minutes soaking
Total cooking time:
  25 minutes
Makes 12 regular muffins

^{1}/2 cup (60 g) raisins
^{1}/2 cup (125 ml) orange
  juice
2^1/2 cups (310 g) self-
  raising flour
^{1}/2 teaspoon
  bicarbonate of soda
^{1}/2 teaspoon freshly
  grated nutmeg
1 cup (100 g) rolled oats
^{3}/4 cup (185 ml)
  buttermilk
2 eggs
^{1}/2 cup (175 g) honey,
  warmed
^{1}/2 cup (125 ml) oil
1 cup (240 g) mashed
  ripe bananas

1. Soak the raisins in the juice for 15 minutes.
2. Preheat the oven to moderate 180°C (350°F/ Gas 4). Line 12 regular muffin holes with muffin papers. Sift the flour, bicarbonate of soda and nutmeg into a bowl. Stir in the oats. Make a well in the centre.
3. Place the buttermilk, eggs, honey and oil in another bowl and

lightly whisk. Stir in the banana and raisins. Pour into the well. Fold until combined—the batter should be lumpy.
4. Divide the batter among the muffin holes. Bake for 20–25 minutes, or until golden. Cool slightly, then transfer to a wire rack. Spread with butter or marmalade.

NUTRITION PER MUFFIN
Protein 5.5 g; Fat 12 g; Carbohydrate 45 g; Dietary Fibre 2.5 g; Cholesterol 30 mg; 1295 kJ (310 cal)

Gooey dark chocolate muffins

Preparation time:
  20 minutes
Total cooking time:
  20 minutes
Makes 6 Texas muffins

150 g dark chocolate,
  chopped
125 g butter, chopped
1^3/4 cups (215 g) self-
  raising flour
^{1}/4 teaspoon baking
  powder
^{1}/4 cup (30 g) cocoa
  powder
^{1}/4 cup (55 g) firmly
  packed soft brown
  sugar
^{3}/4 cup (185 ml) milk
2 eggs
6 Swiss chocolates with
  soft chocolate filling
icing sugar, to dust

1. Preheat the oven to moderately hot 190°C (375°F/Gas 5). Grease 6 Texas muffin holes. Place the chocolate and butter in a heatproof bowl. Bring a saucepan of water to the boil, then remove the pan from the heat. Sit the bowl over the saucepan, making sure the base of the bowl does not sit in the water. Stir occasionally until the chocolate and butter have melted. Remove from the heat.
2. Sift the flour, baking powder and cocoa into a large bowl and stir in the sugar. Make a well in the centre. Place the milk and eggs in a jug, whisk together and pour into the well, then pour in the chocolate mixture. Fold gently until combined—the batter should be lumpy.
3. Divide half the mixture among the muffin holes, top with a chocolate and cover with the remaining batter. Bake for 20 minutes, or until the muffins have come away slightly from the side of the tin. Cool for 10 minutes, then transfer to a wire rack. Dust with icing sugar and serve warm.

NUTRITION PER MUFFIN
Protein 8.5 g; Fat 30 g; Carbohydrate 56 g; Dietary Fibre 2 g; Cholesterol 115 mg; 2145 kJ (513 cal)

Gooey dark chocolate muffins (top) and Banana, oat and raisin muffins

White chocolate and blackberry muffins

Preparation time:
  20 minutes
Total cooking time:
  25 minutes
Makes 12 regular muffins

2¹/2 cups (310 g) self-
  raising flour
¹/2 cup (90 g) white
  choc bits or chopped
  white chocolate melts
¹/2 cup (75 g) white
  chocolate melts
125 g butter
¹/2 cup (95 g) soft
  brown sugar
¹/2 cup (125 ml) milk
3 eggs
300 g blackberries

1. Preheat the oven to moderately hot 200°C (400°F/Gas 6). Grease 12 regular muffin holes. Sift the flour into a bowl and stir in the choc bits. Make a well in the centre.
2. Place the melts and butter in a heatproof bowl. Bring a saucepan of water to the boil, then remove from the heat. Sit the bowl over the pan, making sure it does not touch the water. Stir occasionally until the chocolate melts. Remove from the heat and cool slightly. Add the sugar and milk and beat with electric beaters until well mixed. Whisk in the eggs, then pour into the well in the dry ingredients.
3. Fold together gently, then add the berries. Do not overmix—the batter should be lumpy.
4. Divide the batter among the muffin holes. Bake for 20–25 minutes, or until they come away from the side of the tin. Cool briefly, then transfer to a wire rack.

NUTRITION PER MUFFIN
Protein 5.5 g; Fat 14 g; Carbohydrate 40 g; Dietary Fibre 2 g; Cholesterol 74 mg; 1253 kJ (300 cal)

Banana muffins with caramel syrup

Preparation time:
  15 minutes
Total cooking time:
  25 minutes
Makes 12 regular muffins

2 cups (250 g) self-
  raising flour
¹/2 cup (125 g) caster
  sugar
1 cup (250 ml) milk
1 egg
2 teaspoons vanilla
  essence
75 g unsalted butter,
  melted and cooled
1 cup (240 g) mashed
  ripe banana
1 cup (250 g) sugar

1. Preheat the oven to moderately hot 200°C (400°F/Gas 6). Grease 12 regular muffin holes. Sift the flour into a bowl and stir in the caster sugar. Make a well in the centre.
2. Put the milk, egg and vanilla in a jug, whisk and pour into the well. Add the butter and banana. Fold until combined—the batter should be lumpy.
3. Divide among the muffin holes. Bake for 20–25 minutes, or until the muffins come away from the side of the tin.
4. Meanwhile, to make the syrup, put the sugar and ¹/2 cup (125 ml) water in a small saucepan and stir over medium heat until the sugar dissolves. Increase the heat and cook for 8 minutes, or until golden. Remove from the heat and add ¹/3 cup (80 ml) water (careful—it will spit). Stir the water into the caramel until smooth. Remove from the heat and leave until needed.
5. Cool the muffins for 5 minutes, then transfer to a wire rack. Serve drizzled with the syrup.

NUTRITION PER MUFFIN
Protein 3 g; Fat 6 g; Carbohydrate 50 g; Dietary Fibre 1 g; Cholesterol 20 mg; 1123 kJ (270 cal)

Banana muffins with caramel syrup (top) and White chocolate and blackberry muffins

Spiced Christmas muffins

Preparation time:
  20 minutes + 2 hours marinating
Total cooking time:
  20 minutes
Makes 12 regular muffins

1³/4 cups (325 g) mixed dried fruit
1/3 cup (80 ml) rum or brandy
2¹/2 cups (310 g) self-raising flour
1 teaspoon mixed spice
1 teaspoon ground cinnamon
1/2 teaspoon ground nutmeg
2/3 cup (155 g) firmly packed soft brown sugar
1/2 cup (125 ml) milk
1 egg, lightly beaten
2 tablespoons apricot jam
1/2 teaspoon very finely grated lemon rind
1/2 teaspoon very finely grated orange rind
125 g unsalted butter, melted and cooled
icing sugar, to dust
125 g soft ready-made icing (see Note)
2 tablespoons apricot jam, extra, warmed and sieved
red and green glacé cherries, for decoration

1. Place the mixed dried fruit and rum in a large bowl and mix together. Cover and marinate, stirring often, for 1–2 hours, or until the rum has been completely absorbed by the fruit.
2. Preheat the oven to moderately hot 200°C (400°F/Gas 6). Line 12 regular muffin holes with muffin papers. Sift the flour, mixed spice, cinnamon and nutmeg into a large bowl and stir in the brown sugar. Make a well in the centre.
3. Put the milk, egg, apricot jam, lemon and orange rinds and melted butter in a jug, mix together and pour into the well in the dry ingredients. Stir in the marinated dried fruit mixture. Fold gently until just combined—the batter should be lumpy.
4. Divide the mixture evenly among the muffin holes. Bake for 20 minutes, or until a skewer inserted in the middle of the muffins comes out clean. Cool in the tins for 5 minutes, then transfer the muffins to a wire rack to cool completely.
5. Place the ready-made icing on a work surface dusted with a little icing sugar. Roll out to a thickness of about 2 mm and, using a 7 cm fluted round cutter, cut out 12 rounds from the icing. Reroll the scraps of icing if necessary.
6. Brush the tops of the cooled muffins lightly with the extra apricot jam and place a round of icing on top of each muffin. Decorate with whole or halved red glacé cherries and small pieces of green glacé cherries to represent leaves.

NUTRITION PER MUFFIN
Protein 4 g; Fat 10 g; Carbohydrate 50 g; Dietary Fibre 2.5 g; Cholesterol 43 mg; 1501 kJ (358 cal)

Notes: Before grating the rind of lemons, scrub well using a vegetable brush to remove any wax and pesticide residue. Dry very well before grating.

   Ready-made icing is available in the supermarket in the sugar aisle. It comes in a firm block and requires kneading to make it a pliable consistency. It can be rolled and cut to any shape you like.
Variation: If you like the flavour of these muffins, and can't wait until Christmas, simply replace the cherries with sugar-coated lollies of your choice.

Spiced Christmas muffins

Low-fat muffins

All these low-fat recipes make 12 regular muffins. Preheat the oven to moderately hot 200°C (400°F/Gas 6) and spray 12 regular muffin holes with oil spray or line with muffin papers.

Apple, bran and cinnamon muffins

Sift 2 cups (250 g) self-raising flour and 1$^{1}/_{2}$ teaspoons ground cinnamon into a bowl and stir in $^{1}/_{2}$ cup (75 g) oat bran. Add 1 peeled, cored and chopped green apple. Make a well in the centre.

Stir 30 g unsalted butter and $^{1}/_{2}$ cup (175 g) golden syrup together in a small saucepan over low heat until the butter melts, then cool.

Combine the butter mixture, 1 egg, $^{3}/_{4}$ cup (185 ml) skim milk and $^{1}/_{2}$ cup (125 ml) apple purée in a bowl, mix together and add to the dry ingredients. Fold until combined—the batter should be lumpy.

Divide among the muffin holes. Decorate with small slices of unpeeled apple. Bake for 20 minutes, or until the muffins come away from the side of the tin. Cool briefly, then transfer to a wire rack.
Fat: 3 g per muffin.

Dried fruit and ricotta muffins

Heat $^{3}/_{4}$ cup (140 g) fruit medley and $^{1}/_{2}$ cup (125 ml) orange juice in a small saucepan over low heat for 5 minutes, or until the juice is absorbed. Remove from the heat and cool.

Sift 1$^{3}/_{4}$ cups (215 g) self-raising flour into a large bowl and stir in $^{1}/_{2}$ cup (50 g) rolled oats and $^{1}/_{4}$ cup (55 g) firmly packed soft brown sugar. Make a well in the centre. Stir $^{1}/_{4}$ cup (80 g) apricot jam, $^{3}/_{4}$ cup (185 ml) skim milk, 30 g melted and cooled unsalted butter, 2 teaspoons grated orange rind and 1 lightly beaten egg into the fruit mixture and add to the dry ingredients. Fold until combined—the batter should be lumpy.

Divide among the muffin holes. Cut 125 g low-fat ricotta into 12 pieces. Press into the centre of the muffins.

Sprinkle with sugar. Bake for 20 minutes, or until the muffins come away from the side of the tin. Cool for 5 minutes, then transfer to a wire rack.
Fat: 4 g per muffin.

Banana, honey and nut muffins

Sift 2 cups (250 g) self-raising flour, 1/2 cup (75 g) wholemeal plain flour, 1 teaspoon baking powder and 1 teaspoon each of ground cinnamon and mixed spice into a large bowl and return the husks to the bowl. Stir in 1 tablespoon roasted chopped hazelnuts and 1 tablespoon toasted slivered almonds and make a well in the centre.

Combine 1/3 cup (115 g) honey, 2 tablespoons oil, 1 cup (240 g) mashed ripe banana, 220 g drained tinned apple chunks, 1 egg and 3/4 cup (185 ml) skim milk in a bowl, mix together and add to the dry ingredients. Fold gently until just combined—the batter should be lumpy.

Divide evenly among the muffin holes. Bake for 20 minutes, or until the muffins come away from the side of the tin. Cool briefly, then transfer to a wire rack.
Fat: 4.5 g per muffin.

Rhubarb and custard muffins

Combine 3/4 cup (185 g) caster sugar and 1 cup (250 ml) water in a saucepan and stir over medium heat until the sugar has dissolved.

Add 300 g chopped rhubarb and cook over low heat for 2 minutes, or until tender but not falling apart. Transfer to a bowl and cool—do not stir. Drain, being careful not to break up the rhubarb.

Sift 2 1/4 cups (280 g) self-raising flour and 3/4 cup (90 g) custard powder into a bowl, stir in 1/2 cup (125 g) caster sugar and make a well in the centre.

Combine 1 egg, 30 g melted and cooled unsalted butter and 1 cup (250 ml) skim milk and add to the dry ingredients. Fold gently until just combined—the batter should be lumpy. Fold in the rhubarb.

Divide the mixture among the muffin holes. Sprinkle with sugar and bake for 20–25 minutes, or until golden. Cool for 5 minutes, then transfer to a wire rack.
Fat: 3 g per muffin.

From left: Apple, bran & cinnamon; Dried fruit & ricotta; Banana, honey & nut; Rhubarb & custard.

Blue cheese and pear muffins

Preparation time:
10 minutes
Total cooking time:
25 minutes
Makes 12 regular muffins

1 large ripe pear
2¹/2 cups (310 g) self-raising flour
²/3 cup (85 g) chopped pecans
125 g crumbly blue cheese
1¹/4 cups (315 ml) buttermilk
2 eggs, lightly beaten
¹/3 cup (80 ml) oil
12 pecans, extra

1. Preheat the oven to moderately hot 200°C (400°F/Gas 6). Grease 12 regular muffin holes. Peel, core and finely chop the pear.
2. Sift the flour into a bowl and mix in the pear and pecans. Make a well in the centre.
3. Place the cheese in a separate bowl and mash with a fork, then gradually add the buttermilk, stirring until smooth. Stir in the eggs and oil. Pour into the well in the dry ingredients. Fold gently until just combined—the batter should be lumpy.
4. Divide the mixture evenly among the muffin holes. Place a pecan on the top of each uncooked muffin. Bake for 20–25 minutes, or until the muffins come away slightly from the side of the tin. Cool for 5 minutes, then transfer to a wire rack.

NUTRITION PER MUFFIN
Protein 8 g; Fat 18 g; Carbohydrate 22 g; Dietary Fibre 2 g; Cholesterol 43 mg; 1185 kJ (283 cal)

Peanut butter and sour cream muffins

Preparation time:
20 minutes
Total cooking time:
25 minutes
Makes 6 Texas muffins

12 sugar cubes
¹/2 cup (80 g) roughly chopped roasted unsalted peanuts,
2¹/4 cups (280 g) self-raising flour
¹/2 cup (125 g) caster sugar
¹/2 cup (125 g) crunchy peanut butter
³/4 cup (185 g) sour cream
³/4 cup (185 ml) milk
2 eggs
90 g unsalted butter, melted and cooled
²/3 cup (160 g) sour cream, extra

1. Preheat the oven to moderately hot 200°C (400°F/Gas 6). Grease 6 Texas muffin holes. Line each muffin hole with a 15 cm square of brown paper, roughly pleating it and pushing it into the muffin hole.
2. Lightly crush the sugar cubes in a plastic bag into medium-sized pieces, then put in a small bowl. Add the peanuts and stir.
3. Sift the flour into a bowl and stir in the caster sugar. Make a well in the centre.
4. Place the peanut butter, sour cream, milk, eggs and butter in a jug, mix together and pour into the well. Fold gently until just combined—the batter should be lumpy.
5. Divide half the batter among the muffin holes. Top each with 1 heaped tablespoon of the extra sour cream and spoon the remaining batter evenly over the top, then sprinkle with the peanut mixture.
6. Bake the muffins for 20–25 minutes, or until golden. Cool for 5 minutes, then transfer to a wire rack.

NUTRITION PER MUFFIN
Protein 18 g; Fat 56 g; Carbohydrate 62 g; Dietary Fibre 5 g; Cholesterol 177 mg; 3423 kJ (818 cal)

Peanut butter and sour cream muffins (top) and Blue cheese and pear muffins

Smoked salmon and cream cheese muffins

Preparation time:
  15 minutes
Total cooking time:
  25 minutes
Makes 12 regular muffins

2²/3 cups (335 g) self-raising flour
¹/2 teaspoon baking powder
¹/2 cup (125 g) cream cheese
2 eggs
1²/3 cups (410 ml) milk
2 tablespoons lemon juice
60 g butter, melted and cooled
100 g sliced smoked salmon, cut into thin strips
1 tablespoon finely chopped fresh dill

1. Preheat the oven to moderately hot 190°C (375°F/Gas 5). Grease 12 regular muffin holes. Sift the flour and baking powder into a large bowl and make a well in the centre.
2. Put the cream cheese in a bowl and beat until softened. Beat in the eggs, then the milk. Pour the mixture into the well in the dry ingredients. Add the lemon juice, melted butter, smoked salmon and dill. Fold gently until just combined—the batter should be lumpy.
3. Divide the mixture evenly among the muffin holes and bake for 25 minutes, or until the muffins come away slightly from the side of the tin. Cool briefly, then transfer to a wire rack to cool completely.

NUTRITION PER MUFFIN
Protein 17 g; Fat 30 g; Carbohydrate 33 g; Dietary Fibre 2 g; Cholesterol 140 mg; 1910 kJ (455 cal)

Parmesan, pumpkin and zucchini muffins

Preparation time:
  30 minutes
Total cooking time:
  45 minutes
Makes 6 Texas muffins

200 g pumpkin, peeled and roughly chopped
2 cups (250 g) self-raising flour
¹/2 teaspoon baking powder
³/4 cup (75 g) grated Parmesan
1 zucchini, grated
125 g butter, melted and cooled
1 egg
200 ml milk
1 tablespoon sesame seeds
2–3 tablespoons grated Parmesan, extra

1. Preheat the oven to moderately hot 190°C (375°F/Gas 5). Line 6 Texas muffin holes with muffin papers. Steam the pumpkin for 10 minutes, or until tender. Mash until smooth, then cool.
2. Sift the flour and baking powder into a large bowl, then mix in the Parmesan. Make a well in the centre.
3. Place the pumpkin, zucchini and butter in a separate bowl. Beat the egg and milk together in a jug and pour into the pumpkin mixture. Mix together.
4. Pour into the well in the dry ingredients. Fold gently until just combined—the batter should be lumpy.
5. Divide the muffin mixture evenly among the muffin holes and sprinkle with the sesame seeds and extra grated Parmesan.
6. Bake for 35 minutes, or until a skewer inserted in the middle comes out clean. Cool for 5 minutes, then transfer to a wire rack.

NUTRITION PER MUFFIN
Protein 7.5 g; Fat 10 g; Carbohydrate 22 g; Dietary Fibre 1 g; Cholesterol 60 mg; 887 kJ (212 cal)

Parmesan, pumpkin and zucchini muffins (top) and Smoked salmon and cream cheese muffins

Spinach and feta muffins

Preparation time:
  25 minutes
Total cooking time:
  30 minutes
Makes 6 Texas muffins

185 g English spinach
  leaves
2^{1}/2 cups (310 g) self-
  raising flour
^{1}/2 teaspoon paprika
125 g feta, crumbled
4 spring onions, finely
  chopped
1 tablespoon chopped
  fresh dill
1 cup (250 ml)
  buttermilk
1 egg, lightly beaten
^{1}/3 cup (80 ml) olive oil
60 g feta, crumbled,
  extra

1. Preheat the oven to
moderately hot 200°C
(400°F/Gas 6). Grease
6 Texas muffin holes.
Steam the spinach until
just tender. Drain and
squeeze out any excess
liquid. Chop finely.
2. Sift the flour and
paprika into a bowl and
stir in the feta,
spring onion and dill.
Make a well in the
centre. Pour in the
combined buttermilk,
egg and oil, then add
the spinach. Fold gently
until combined—the
batter should be lumpy.
3. Divide the mixture
evenly among the
muffin holes. Sprinkle
the extra feta over
the top and bake for
25–30 minutes, or
until golden. Cool for
5 minutes, then transfer
to a wire rack.

NUTRITION PER MUFFIN
*Protein 14 g; Fat 22 g;
Carbohydrate 40 g; Dietary
Fibre 3 g; Cholesterol
55 mg; 1740 kJ (416 cal)*

Bacon and egg muffins

Preparation time:
  20 minutes
Total cooking time:
  30 minutes
Makes 6 Texas muffins

3 rashers bacon, finely
  chopped
2 hard-boiled eggs,
  chopped
2 cups (250 g) plain
  flour
1 tablespoon baking
  powder
2 tablespoons sugar
pinch cayenne pepper
1 teaspoon dry mustard
^{3}/4 cup (90 g) grated
  strong Cheddar
^{3}/4 cup (185 ml) milk
1 egg
^{1}/4 cup (60 ml) oil
50 g grated Cheddar,
  extra

1. Preheat the oven to
moderately hot 200°C
(400°F/Gas 6). Grease
6 Texas muffin holes.
Place the bacon in a
frying pan and cook,
stirring, over medium
heat for 3–5 minutes, or
until golden. Drain on
paper towels. Transfer
to a small bowl and mix
with the chopped egg.
2. Sift the flour and
baking powder into a
bowl and stir in the
sugar, cayenne pepper,
mustard, Cheddar and
^{1}/2 teaspoon salt. Make
a well in the centre.
3. Place the milk, egg
and oil in a jug, whisk
together and pour into
the well. Fold gently
until combined—the
batter should be lumpy.
4. Fill each muffin hole
one third full with the
mixture, forming a
slight indentation in the
centre of each. Divide
the egg and bacon
filling among the tins,
keeping it piled in the
middle. Top with the
remaining batter.
5. Sprinkle the extra
Cheddar over the
top, then bake for
20–25 minutes, or until
the muffins are risen
and golden. Cool in the
tin for 5 minutes, then
transfer to a wire rack
to cool completely.

NUTRITION PER MUFFIN
*Protein 18 g; Fat 22 g;
Carbohydrate 40 g; Dietary
Fibre 1.5 g; Cholesterol
127 mg; 1789 kJ (427 cal)*

*Spinach and feta muffins (top) and
Bacon and egg muffins*

Tomato, bocconcini and basil muffins

Preparation time:
  10 minutes
Total cooking time:
  25 minutes
Makes 12 regular muffins

2³/4 cups (340 g) self-
  raising flour
1/2 teaspoon baking
  powder
1 1/2 cups (375 ml) milk
2 eggs, beaten
2 Roma tomatoes,
  chopped
3 bocconcini, chopped
3 tablespoons shredded
  fresh basil
60 g butter, melted and
  cooled

1. Preheat the oven to moderately hot 200°C (400°F/Gas 6). Grease 12 regular muffin holes. Sift the flour and baking powder into a large bowl and stir in 1/4 teaspoon salt and 1/4 teaspoon cracked black pepper. Make a well in the centre.
2. Whisk the milk and eggs together in a jug, then pour into the well. Add the tomato, bocconcini, basil and melted butter and mix together well. Fold gently until just combined—the mixture should be lumpy.
3. Divide the batter evenly among the muffin holes and bake for 25 minutes, or until the muffins come away slightly from the side of the tin. Cool in the tin for 5 minutes, then transfer to a wire rack. Best served warm. These are great with piping hot soup.

NUTRITION PER MUFFIN
Protein 7.5 g; Fat 8.5 g; Carbohydrate 22 g; Dietary Fibre 1 g; Cholesterol 53 mg; 811 kJ (194 cal)

Corn and chilli muffins

Preparation time:
  10 minutes
Total cooking time:
  25 minutes
Makes 6 Texas muffins

1 red bird's-eye chilli
  (see Note)
1 red banana chilli
  (see Note)
2 cups (250 g) self-
  raising flour
1/2 cup (125 g) sour
  cream
1 cup (250 ml) milk
1 egg
1/3 cup (80 ml) oil
1 cup (200 g) corn
  kernels
2 tablespoons chopped
  fresh coriander leaves

1. Preheat the oven to moderate 180°C (350°F/Gas 4). Grease 6 Texas muffin holes. Remove the seeds and membrane from both chillies and chop finely.
2. Sift the flour into a large bowl, then add 1/4 teaspoon salt and 1/4 teaspoon cracked black pepper and make a well in the centre.
3. Combine the sour cream, milk, egg and oil in a bowl and mix together. Stir in the corn, both chillies and the coriander. Pour into the well in the dry ingredients. Fold gently until just combined—the batter should be lumpy.
4. Divide the mixture evenly among the muffin holes. Bake for about 20–25 minutes, or until the muffins come away slightly from the side of the tin. Cool for 5 minutes, then transfer to a wire rack to cool completely.

NUTRITION PER MUFFIN
Protein 7.5 g; Fat 24 g; Carbohydrate 38 g; Dietary Fibre 3 g; Cholesterol 62 mg; 1657 kJ (395 cal)

Note: The heat in chillies is contained in the seeds and membrane—if you are a chilli lover, you can leave the seeds and membrane in the chillies for a hot and fiery muffin.

*Corn and chilli muffins (top) and
Tomato, bocconcini and basil muffins*

Mushroom, Parmesan and basil muffins

Preparation time:
  10 minutes
Total cooking time:
  25 minutes
Makes 12 regular muffins

2^1/2 cups (310 g) self-raising flour
^{2}/3 cup (65 g) grated Parmesan
3 tablespoons finely shredded fresh basil
250 g Swiss brown mushrooms, finely chopped
1^1/4 cups (315 ml) milk
1 egg, lightly beaten
^{1}/3 cup (80 ml) olive oil
6 Swiss brown mushrooms, sliced, extra

1. Preheat the oven to moderately hot 200°C (400°F/Gas 6). Grease 12 regular muffin holes. Sift the flour into a bowl and add the cheese, basil and mushrooms. Make a well in the centre.
2. Place the milk, egg and oil in a jug, whisk together and pour into the well. Fold gently until combined—the batter should be lumpy.
3. Divide the mixture evenly among the muffin holes. Top with a few slices of the extra mushroom. Bake for 20–25 minutes, or until the muffins come away from the side of the tin. Cool briefly, then transfer to a wire rack.

NUTRITION PER MUFFIN
Protein 12 g; Fat 16 g; Carbohydrate 20 g; Dietary Fibre 1 g; Cholesterol 43 mg; 1134 kJ (270 cal)

Ratatouille muffins

Preparation time:
  20 minutes +
  cooling time
Total cooking time:
  40 minutes
Makes 10 regular muffins

1 large Roma tomato, halved and deseeded
^{1}/2 zucchini
^{1}/4 eggplant
^{1}/4 red capsicum
^{1}/4 red onion
^{1}/2 teaspoon dried basil
^{1}/2 teaspoon dried oregano
1 tablespoon olive oil
2^1/4 cups (280 g) self-raising flour
1 cup (250 ml) milk
1 egg, lightly beaten
90 g butter, melted and cooled
^{1}/2 cup (100 g) semi-dried tomatoes, chopped
1 teaspoon sea salt
^{1}/2 teaspoon dried oregano, extra

1. Preheat the oven to moderately hot 200°C (400°F/Gas 6). Grease 10 regular muffin holes. Chop the tomato, zucchini, eggplant, capsicum and onion into 5 mm dice. Place in a small baking tin and sprinkle with the dried herbs and some salt and pepper, then drizzle with the oil, stirring to coat. Roast for 20 minutes, or until soft. Cool. (Leave the oven on.)
2. Sift the flour into a large bowl and make a well in the centre.
3. Whisk the milk, egg and butter together in a bowl, then fold in the roasted vegetables and all except 10 pieces of the semi-dried tomatoes. Pour into the well. Fold until combined—the batter should be lumpy.
4. Divide the mixture among the muffin holes and sprinkle with the combined sea salt and oregano, then top with the reserved semi-dried tomatoes. Bake for 20 minutes, or until the muffins come away from the side of the tin. Cool for 5 minutes, then transfer to a wire rack.

NUTRITION PER MUFFIN
Protein 4.5 g; Fat 11 g; Carbohydrate 22 g; Dietary Fibre 1.5 g; Cholesterol 44 mg; 862 kJ (206 cal)

Mushroom, Parmesan and basil muffins (top) and Ratatouille muffins

Olive and thyme muffins

Preparation time:
  20 minutes
Total cooking time:
  20 minutes
Makes 12 regular muffins

3 cups (375 g) self-
  raising flour
$^1/_3$ cup (35 g) grated
  Parmesan
$^3/_4$ cup (140 g) mixed
  black and green
  chopped olives
3 tablespoons fresh
  thyme leaves
$1^1/_2$ cups (375 ml) milk
2 eggs
$^1/_4$ cup (60 ml) olive oil
12 tips fresh thyme, to
  garnish (optional)

1. Preheat the oven
to moderate 180°C
(350°F/Gas 4). Grease
12 regular muffin
holes. Sift the flour
and $^1/_2$ teaspoon salt
into a bowl. Add the
Parmesan, olives and
thyme and stir together.
Make a well in the
centre.
2. Lightly whisk
together the milk, eggs
and oil in a jug and
pour into the well.
Fold gently until just
combined—the batter
should be lumpy.
3. Divide the mixture
evenly among the
muffin holes. If desired,
place a thyme tip on
top of the muffins for
garnish. Bake for
20 minutes, or until
muffins come away
from the side of the tin.
Cool for 5 minutes,
then transfer to a wire
rack to cool completely.

NUTRITION PER MUFFIN
*Protein 6 g; Fat 8 g;
Carbohydrate 24 g; Dietary
Fibre 2 g; Cholesterol
22 mg; 811 kJ (195 cal)*

Caramelised onion muffins

Preparation time:
  25 minutes
Total cooking time:
  50 minutes
Makes 6 Texas muffins

30 g butter
2 small onions, sliced
3–4 tablespoons
  chopped fresh sage
1 tablespoon soft
  brown sugar
2 cups (250 g) self-
  raising flour
$1^1/_3$ cups (150 g)
  ground almonds
$1^3/_4$ cups (440 ml) milk
1 egg
1 teaspoon olive oil
12 sage leaves

1. Preheat the oven
to moderate 180°C
(350°F/Gas 4). Grease
6 Texas muffin holes.
Line each muffin hole
with a 15 cm square of
brown paper, roughly
pleating it and pushing
it into the muffin hole.
2. Melt the butter
in a frying pan, add
the onion and cook,
stirring, over medium
heat for 15–20 minutes,
or until very soft. Add
the chopped sage and
brown sugar and cook,
stirring, for 2 minutes.
Cool.
3. Sift the flour into a
large bowl, stir in the
ground almonds and
season with salt and
pepper. Make a well in
the centre. Combine the
milk, egg and oil in a
jug and mix together.
Pour into the well, then
stir in three-quarters
of the onion mixture.
Fold gently until just
combined—the batter
should be lumpy.
4. Spoon the mixture
into the muffin holes,
top with the remaining
onion mixture and
decorate with a sage
leaf, tucking the corner
of the leaf under the
onion mixture. Bake
for 20–25 minutes,
or until the muffins
are risen and golden
brown. Cool for
5 minutes, then transfer
to a wire rack to cool
completely.

NUTRITION PER MUFFIN
*Protein 13 g; Fat 23 g;
Carbohydrate 3 g; Dietary
Fibre 4 g; Cholesterol
53 mg; 1708 kJ (408 cal)*

*Caramelised onion muffins (top) and
Olive and thyme muffins*

Three cheese muffins

Preparation time:
  20 minutes
Total cooking time:
  20 minutes
Makes 10 regular muffins

75 g goat's milk cheese
3 tablespoons finely
  chopped fresh flat-leaf
  parsley
2¹/2 cups (310 g) self-
  raising flour
1 cup (125 g) grated
  Cheddar
²/3 cup (65 g) finely
  grated Parmesan
1¹/4 cups (315 ml) milk
1 egg
80 g butter, melted and
  cooled

1. Preheat the oven to moderate 180°C (350°F/Gas 4). Grease 10 regular muffin holes. Cut the goat's milk cheese into 10 pieces, then roll it in the parsley until evenly coated.
2. Sift the flour and ¹/2 teaspoon salt into a bowl and stir in the Cheddar and Parmesan. Season, then make a well in the centre.
3. Lightly whisk together the milk, egg and butter in a jug and pour into the well. Fold until combined—the batter should be lumpy.
4. Divide the mixture among the muffin holes. Top each muffin with a piece of herbed goat's milk cheese. Bake for 20 minutes, or until golden. Cool for 5 minutes, then transfer to a wire rack.

NUTRITION PER MUFFIN
*Protein 12 g; Fat 17 g;
Carbohydrate 24 g; Dietary
Fibre 1 g; Cholesterol
67 mg; 1218 kJ (291 cal)*

Olive muffins with a crunchy Parmesan topping

Preparation time:
  25 minutes
Total cooking time:
  30 minutes
Makes 12 regular muffins

Topping
¹/2 cup (40 g) fresh
  white breadcrumbs
¹/4 cup (25 g) grated
  Parmesan
30 g butter, melted

2 tablespoons olive oil
1 small red onion,
  finely chopped
2¹/2 cups (310 g) self-
  raising flour
1 cup (250 ml) milk
2 eggs
²/3 cup (100 g) black
  olives, chopped
100 g chargrilled red
  capsicum, finely
  chopped
60 g butter, melted and
  cooled

1. Preheat the oven to moderately hot 200°C (400°F/Gas 6). Grease 12 regular muffin holes. To make the topping, place the breadcrumbs and Parmesan in a small bowl and stir in the melted butter until well mixed.
2. Heat the oil in a small frying pan. Cook the onion over medium heat for 3 minutes, or until softened. Cool slightly.
3. Sift the flour into a large bowl. Make a well in the centre. Place the milk, eggs and onion (including any oil from the pan) in a jug, whisk together and pour into the well. Add the olives, chargrilled capsicum and melted butter. Fold gently until just combined—the batter should be lumpy.
4. Divide the muffin mixture evenly among the muffin holes and evenly sprinkle each muffin with the topping. Bake for 20–25 minutes, or until the muffins come away slightly from the side of the tin. Cool for 5 minutes, then transfer to a wire rack.

NUTRITION PER MUFFIN
*Protein 6 g; Fat 12 g;
Carbohydrate 22 g; Dietary
Fibre 1.5 g; Cholesterol
54 mg; 941 kJ (225 cal)*

*Three cheese muffins (top) and
Olive muffins with a crunchy Parmesan topping*

Index

Almond, berry & yoghurt muffins, 16
almond muffins with citrus syrup, Orange &, 39
Apple & berry crumble muffins, 4
Apple, bran & cinnamon muffins, 48
Apple & cinnamon muffins, 25
Apple muffins with a walnut streusel topping, 34
Apricot & pecan muffins, 11

Bacon & egg muffins, 54
Banana, honey & nut muffins, 49
Banana muffins with caramel syrup, 44
Banana, oat & raisin muffins, 43
berry & yoghurt muffins, Almond, 16
Berry bran muffins with honey butter, 34
berry crumble muffins, Apple &, 4
blackberry muffins, White chocolate &, 44
Blue cheese & pear muffins, 50
Blueberry muffins, 24
bocconcini & basil muffins, Tomato, 57
Bran muffins, 24
bran muffins, Pear & hazelnut, 23
bran muffins with honey butter, Berry, 34

Cappuccino ice cream muffins, 19
caramel syrup, Banana muffins with, 44
Caramelised onion muffins, 61
carrot muffins, Orange-frosted, 7
cheese muffins, Three, 62
chilli muffins, Corn &, 57
chocolate & blackberry muffins, White, 44
chocolate chip muffins, Double, 39
Chocolate muffins, 25
chocolate muffins, Gooey dark, 43
Chocolate muffins with a cream cheese centre, 16
Christmas muffins, Spiced, 47
coconut muffins, Lime &, 15
Coffee nut muffins, 7
Corn & chilli muffins, 57

cream cheese muffins, Smoked salmon &, 53
custard muffins, Rhubarb &, 49

date muffins, Marsala, 29
date muffins, Sticky, 12
Double chocolate chip muffins, 39
Dried fruit & ricotta muffins, 48–9

Ebony & ivory muffins, 30
egg muffins, Bacon &, 54

feta muffins, Spinach &, 54
Fig & oat bran muffins, 12

gingerbread muffins, Sticky, 40
glazes, 37
golden syrup muffins, Oat &, 23

hazelnut bran muffins, Pear &, 23
Hot cross muffins, 15
Hummingbird muffins, 20

ice cream muffins, Strawberry &, 30
icings & toppings, 36–7

Jam-filled muffins, 11

Lemon & poppy seed muffins, 8
Lemon meringue muffins, 33
Lemon syrup muffins, 26
Lime & coconut muffins, 15
low-fat muffins, 48–9

Macadamia & mango muffins, 26
mango muffins, Macadamia &, 26
Marsala date muffins, 29
meringue muffins, Lemon, 33
muesli muffins, Pear &, 8
Mushroom, Parmesan & basil muffins, 58

Oat & golden syrup muffins, 23
oat & raisin muffins, Banana, 43
oat bran muffins, Fig &, 12
Olive & thyme muffins, 61

Olive muffins with a crunchy Parmesan topping, 62
onion muffins, Caramelised, 61
Orange & almond muffins with citrus syrup, 39
Orange-frosted carrot muffins, 7

Parmesan & basil muffins, Mushroom, 58
Parmesan, pumpkin & zucchini muffins, 53
Peanut butter & sour cream muffins, 50
Pear & hazelnut bran muffins, 23
Pear & muesli muffins, 8
pear muffins, Blue cheese &, 50
pecan muffins, Apricot &, 11
poppy seed muffins, Lemon &, 8
Pumpkin & walnut muffins, 29
pumpkin & zucchini muffins, Parmesan, 53

raisin muffins, Banana, oat &, 43
Ratatouille muffins, 58
Rhubarb & custard muffins, 49
Rhubarb crumble muffins, 20
Ricotta & dried fruit muffins, 48–9

Smoked salmon & cream cheese muffins, 53
sour cream muffins, Peanut butter &, 50
Spiced Christmas muffins, 47
Spinach & feta muffins, 54
Sticky date muffins, 12
Sticky gingerbread muffins, 40
Strawberry & ice cream muffins, 30

Three cheese muffins, 62
Tomato, bocconcini & basil muffins, 57
toppings, 36–7

walnut muffins, Pumpkin &, 29
White chocolate & blackberry muffins, 44

yoghurt muffins, Almond, berry &, 16

zucchini muffins, Parmesan, pumpkin &, 53